Expectant Parents Workshop

Devotional

Jennifer DeBrito, CCLD, CCBE

ISBN-13:978-1484877814
ISBN-10: 1484877810

Cover photo © 2013 Jessica Newman Photography

DEDICATION

This devotional is dedicated to my beloved family—all of you, whether you are here, overseas, or waiting for me in Heaven. I love you.

And, to all the future families out there. May yours become a reflection of the eternal family to which you already belong.

ACKNOWLEDGEMENTS

My sincerest thanks to Suzanne Gosselin (for your editing and guidance), Dr. Keith Davis at the Center for Biblical Counseling (for your expert opinion and encouragement), Jenny Bender at Newborn Hope (for your ideas and inspiration), Jessica Newman at Jessica Newman Photography (for your photographic talent and endless generosity), Pastor Don Overton at North Springs Alliance Church (for your sound teaching, which resonates throughout this devotional), Carolyn Baran at the Colorado Springs Pregnancy Center/Life Network (for speaking into my personal development, propelling this project forward), and of course, a huge thank you to my beloved husband, Austin (for your participation, honesty, patience, leadership, and logic). Thank you, Mom & Dad, for your boundless belief in me, and Jason Evans, for shaping me into the "thinker" that I am today (may it be known to all that you were the real writer in the family). And of course, my children—my very own little personal rays of sunshine—thank you for helping me to understand God's unconditional love with such unmistakable clarity. Some of my best growing has come because of you two! Thanks to Sarah Wierschke & Grandma Nikki (for your friendship and confidence), and to the countless other friends who have directed my life to the One who saves, heals, loves, and forgives without end. You know who you are. Thank you.

CONTENTS

Preface   *How To Read This Devotional*   *i*

Week 1   (*For Us*)   Why This Time is Important   1
                  (*For Him*)   Man of the House   10
                  (*For Her*)   Building Your Household   20

Week 2   (*For Us*)   Who Stands Where?   31
                  (*For Him*)   To Everything There is a Season   39
                  (*For Her*)   Birth Plan, or Idol?   49
                        (*For Her, Day 2*) Sex and Candy   56

Week 3   (*For Us*)   The Big Day   62
                  (*For Him*)   Her Coach and Her Savior   68
                  (*For Her*)   Birth Stories are God Stories   76

Week 4   (*For Us*)   Sharing Your Birth Story   83
                  (*For Him*)   Whatever is Noble   90
                  (*For Her*)   Postpartum Oppression   100

Quick Reference for During Labor
                  (*For Him*)   WEIGHTS Acronym   71
                  (*For Her*)   Scriptures To Use During Labor   108

Quick Reference for Postpartum Period
                  (*For Him*)   TIME Acronym   94
                  (*For Us*)   Recording Your Child's Birth Story 114

PREFACE
HOW TO READ THIS DEVOTIONAL

Dear Reader,

This is intended as a devotional for you and your spouse to complete together over the course of four weeks. The sooner you can get started, the better—but it's never too late to begin. This devotional is not intended as medical advice and should be completed alongside a qualified childbirth class.

The sections labeled *"For Us"* are intended to be covered and discussed together. The sections separately labeled *"For Him"* and *"For Her"* should be completed separately. **Reading your partner's sections is unnecessary, and possibly even counter-productive**. Try to allow room for God to work on your spouse, without trying to intervene. Have faith in what God can do.

Each section is short and will take little time to read. Try not to rush through; instead, take the time to really ask yourselves the questions that are included. Allow time for God to respond to your questions, your thoughts, and your feelings in the days following your completion of each section. At the end of each section is a short prayer. The prayers are your only homework, and are intended to be prayed each day during the remainder of the week.

May your heart and your marriage become fully prepared for the blessing of parenthood as you grow closer to each other and closer to God.

Jen DeBrito

WEEK 1

(*For Us*)

WHY THIS TIME IS IMPORTANT

"Be alert and of sober mind. Your enemy the devil prowls around like a roaring lion looking for someone to devour." 1 Peter 5:8

My husband and I haven't been married forever. We're both still young (in our early-to-mid 30's) and neither of us even have any gray hair. Not yet, anyway. Still, as we're pushing toward ten years of marriage, I am definitely able to look back and see how we have grown. I remember how when we first got married and talked about having a family, we assumed that the pregnancy stage would be a delightfully easy time in our marriage. It would be perfectly planned and exciting, and everything would be lined up 'just so' for our little children. When we thought about our future family, we fully expected the early stages of pregnancy and parenthood to hold nothing but the most cherished of memories for us.

The cherished memories are most certainly there. The part we were not aware of, however, is that no marriage is immune to difficulty—especially during times of extreme change. This includes

1

your marriage, too. As much as you are probably planning for everything to go perfectly as you and your spouse embark into the uncharted territory of pregnancy, chances are you are going to run into at least a few snags along the way.

Assuming that most of you (although I realize not *all*) are probably fairly new to your marriage, I want you to know that I remember. I remember how tough those first several years can be. I remember what it's like to be learning to live with a spouse, managing relationships with in-laws, figuring out how to manage money, and trying to find where I fit in the midst of all the change—all while feeling hopeful yet unsure about the future. Add a baby to the equation, and the thought of it all can be a little daunting.

Some couples seem to sail effortlessly from the newlywed stage to pregnancy and early parenthood without ever experiencing a single complication with their spouse. If that's you, soak it up, friend! (But try not to brag; it's annoying to the rest of us mere mortals.) For every couple who thinks this time of life is easy, I am willing to bet that there are 5 more who are confused about why this phase of life is proving to be more difficult than they expected.

I will go ahead and admit that my family came dangerously close to being broken a few years ago. I tell you, we were *strug-gling*. We could not seem to make any sense of what was happening to us. In the blink of an eye, it seemed like everything we had hoped for our family started crumbling to pieces. What happened to our dreams of a happy household for our children? What happened to the love and laughter that used to fill our home? It occurred to me during that time that no one who gets married ever thinks they're going to get divorced. And no couple that gets divorced ever thought it would happen to them.

• **In your mind, think of a family you know that is "unhappy" or "broken." Think of the hardships they have endured, and, in the space provided, list out as many traits as you can that describe this family.**

Broken Family:

Look at the list again.

There is someone out there who wants your family to have every single one of the traits on that list. There is someone who wants only the worst for you, his ultimate goal being to somehow get you to give up and separate yourself from your family and from God, just like he did. He hates everything a family stands for and wants nothing more than to break up your family before it even has a chance to start. He wants to hurt you and fill your head with lies. In fact, he is the "father of lies" (John 8:44) and has come "only to steal and kill and destroy" (John 10:10).

With the help of a good counselor, I came to learn that many of the problems we were having as a couple took root during our first year of marriage. For us, that was also the time of my pregnancy with our first child. As our relationship underwent a turbulent flow of changes, we both came to misunderstand each other in numerous ways. We began to believe lies about each other that made us each doubt the other's intentions. We quickly grew apart during what should have been one of the happiest times of our life. We never intended for it to happen that way, but it did.

As a young Christian family, it is important for you to understand how vulnerable you are during this time.

• **Can you see how it would make sense to the enemy, to try to unravel your family before it has a chance to start?**

• **Ask God to help you understand how important this time is for your future family, and ask for His protection as you embark into the territory of parenthood.**

Pregnancy is a time filled with change: hormones, relationships, finances, just to name a few. It is a time when couples can either grow together into a Christ-centered parental unit, or perhaps without even realizing it, grow apart. Your parenthood started the moment your child was conceived. Now is the time to start resisting the enemy so he will flee from your family (James 4:7).

• **Now, in your mind, think of a family which you consider to be "Christ-Centered." While no family is perfect, in the space** below, write down as many characteristics as you can to describe this family.

Christ-Centered Family:

• **Place a (*) next to each quality that you hope your future family will possess, as well as adding any additional ones.**

Look at the list again.

There is One who wants every single one of the traits on that list for your family. There is One who loves you and wants only the best for you, whose ultimate goal for you is to realize that nothing can separate you from God's love (Romans 8:38). He *is* God (John 8:58)—and He has already paid the price for your ticket into His family. He loves everything that a family stands for and cannot wait to be reunited with you in Heaven someday, and to live with you on the new Earth He will someday create.

If you are a believer in Jesus Christ and have accepted Him as your Lord and Savior—if you have decided to accept the ticket He bought for you—then you are part of His family and you will live to see those days! Until then, you are called to show His love to anyone who does not yet know Him. And what better way for your family to show His love than to be a reflection of the family you belong to in Heaven!

**"...I have come that they may have life, and have it to the full."
(John 10:10)**

It is important to understand that try as we may, none of us is capable of creating the kind of family that has the characteristics others would want to put a (*) next to—at least, not on our own. You see, we are imperfect beings and no matter how hard we try as parents, we will create imperfect families. What it comes down to is this: If we want our family to possess the traits of the Christ-centered family, *we must have Christ at the center*!

Choose today what kind of family you are going to raise. Are you going to try to raise your family by your own hands, or by God's? It is a choice you will need to make each day, resisting the urge to try to make things how you think they should be and choosing instead to give God control over your family's future. As you are faced with each opportunity to choose between your own power and God's, you are going to need each other's support and encouragement.

• Take a few minutes to ask God to cover your family with His love, guidance, and protection. Ask Him to help you with the difficult task of giving Him control.

Before we start talking about pregnancy, childbirth, or anything else you *think* will be covered in this devotional, I want you to look at your spouse and say, "We are going to be a family!" Then, for a fun closing activity, take a few minutes to read over "Example House Rules" below. Working together, create a few rules of your own. Consider what you want your child's home life to be like as he or she grows, and let your rules serve as a daily reminder of the kind of Christ-centered family you want to be. Creating a way to display it in the home can also be a fun project for couples as they await the arrival of their new family member.

Example House Rules :
Say I love you. Pray often.
Practice grace.
Dream big.
No yelling.
Be the first to say sorry.
Always tell the truth.
Forgive and recover.
Slow dance in the kitchen.
Work hard.
Hug often.
Consider it pure joy when you face trials. (James 1:2)

Our House Rules:

• Homework: Pray the following prayer together each day this week.

"Lord, thank You for what You have shown us about the importance of this time in our marriage. We pray that You will protect us and help us to grow closer to each other and to You, as we prepare for the arrival of our child. Please help us to remember that we are imperfect, that our family will be imperfect, and that we need You at the center of our household. Lord, we commit our family to You. All the glory is Yours. Thank You for being the Head of our household. In Jesus' name, amen."

WEEK 1

(For Him)

THE MAN OF THE HOUSE

• **When you think of being "man of the house," what comes to mind? What does that term mean to you? List both the positive and the negative.**

When we were dating, my husband Austin and I were a crazy, fun-loving couple. Concerts, camping, and spur-of-the-moment adventures are some of our best memories together from that time. We worked together (which is how we met) and sat just a few desks away from each other. We would IM all day long. We still laugh about how my computer screen would *ding* every time I received a message, because I didn't have the sense to turn off my speakers. We were young and making pretty good money. And quite honestly, we didn't realize how good we had it.

When we returned from our honeymoon in September 2005, we learned that we had both been laid off along with hundreds of others in our workplace. Instead of being concerned, we were thrilled with the generous severance package each of us had received and proceeded to treat the following months as a sort of extended vacation. We did very little to look for new work. (Did I mention we were young?) Each morning felt like a Saturday, complete with egg breakfasts, coffee, and dreaming together about our future. We felt like success was ours for the taking.

In February, I found out I was pregnant.

Suddenly, everything changed for us. While I was dealing with extreme fatigue and morning sickness, Austin was stuck trying to figure out what we were going to do for income and insurance. Our severance packages were about to end, which meant we needed to figure something out fast. I went to work in a call center while he stayed home to seek out a job that would hopefully replace both of our previous incomes. I remember how my body ached at work from early pregnancy symptoms and how I would collapse on the couch upon returning home, emotionally and physically exhausted. Austin took good care of me; he made sure I ate well and kept the house picked up while he stayed home looking for work.

Having been raised in a dual-income family, I was unaware that there was a sort of role reversal taking place in our marriage. Austin, on the other hand, had been raised in a more traditional home and was very aware of it. I learned years later that this period of time was particularly difficult for him.

> **Hey guys, this is Austin. When Jen told me she was pregnant, I was sick to my stomach. I didn't even have a job. How could I afford to have a family?**

• Do you feel prepared to step into your role as the "man of the house"? Why or why not?

"But I want you to realize that the head of every man is Christ, and the head of every woman is man, and the head of Christ is God." 1 Corinthians 11:3

If you are feeling a little overwhelmed by all the responsibilities that assuming your role as man of the house will bring, that is understandable. If you are feeling like my husband felt, and don't feel ready to take on those responsibilities, that is understandable too. There is a lot being asked of you that may not have ever been asked of you before. Add in complications such as unemployment or financial hardships, and suddenly providing for a family can feel overwhelming, confusing, and perhaps even impossible.

Some of you might have been fortunate enough to have a good role model whom you can try to emulate as you move into your new role. Others of you might not have been so lucky. Either way, I have good news for you: As you take on the huge role of becoming the man of your house, you have Someone looking out for you, too. In fact, you have *two levels* of leadership above you that you can count on to share the burden of raising your family. Although it may sometimes feel like it's all up to you, it isn't.

• **Look at 1 Corinthians 11:3 again. Who is the true Head of your household? Ask God to show you the difference between your role in your household, and His. Ask Him to assume His role in your house today.**

Once you trust Christ as the true Head of your household, you might be interested to learn that there are Biblical principles for how to handle your money. I remember what an immense relief it was when Austin told me he wanted to start following the plan outlined in the classes offered at our church. Once we learned and started applying those principles, we finally stopped fighting about money. It didn't fix our financial problems immediately; it has taken patience and commitment on our part, and we still have to be pretty careful with how we spend. But simply being in agreement about what our plan was for ourselves made a huge difference in our relationship. If you haven't yet attended a Biblically-based financial class, you might consider signing up for one—before the baby comes, if possible.

Applying Biblical principles to our finances probably saved our marriage. I only wish we had done it sooner. -Austin

Jesus replied: " 'Love the Lord your God with all your heart and with all your soul and with all your mind.' This is the first and greatest commandment. And the second is like it: 'Love your neighbor as yourself.' " Matthew 22:37-39

While we are talking about roles in the home, it is important to remember that just as it can be difficult for you to remember to look to God as your leader, it can also be difficult for your wife to look to you as hers. It is most people's natural tendency to try to do things in their own way, by their own power. Keep in mind that your wife may also struggle with figuring out her role, and it may take her a while to learn how to embrace you as the head of the household. As you and your wife work to fall into your proper roles as a parental unit under Christ, remember that you are called to treat her as you would like to be treated.

• **Look at Matthew 22:39. Ask God to give you a healthy understanding of the way you and your wife should treat each other.**

"Husbands, love your wives, just as Christ loved the church and gave himself up for her." Ephesians 5:25

I have included a list for you to read, entitled "Notes For Dad." This is a list I made for the first father I ever worked with as a doula. It includes ten ideas for how to be there for your wife during pregnancy. I must admit, it contains a combination of things my own husband did, along with a few things I wished he had known to do.

Every father I have worked with since has also found these tips helpful. You will need to try some of the items more than once; others are practices that should be included in your relationship together from now on.

• **Ask God to help you remember to use the ideas on the "Notes For Dad" list on the following pages.**

Notes For Dad

1) Time in the Word, by yourself. Praying and reading your Bible as you seek God's guidance is the most important thing you can do to care for your wife. So get up early, stay up late, or miss a TV show. Your wife will respect your decision to seek God at this important time in your lives.

2) Time in the Word, together. Pray together. Be the one to initiate it (your wife really wants this). Pick a time of day, such as before breakfast or dinner, or before bed, and make sure it happens. You are the man of the household—so take this important initiative and continue it with your wife from now on.

3) Be the one to initiate doing homework from the childbirth classes you take together. This will show your wife that you care, and that you are interested and excited. It only takes a few minutes, but the benefits are immeasurable.

4) Take an interest in the baby in her belly. If you haven't already, start holding your wife's belly and feeling for movement. You can even talk and sing to her belly. You might feel strange at first; do it anyway. Your wife will love it, and so will the baby.

5) Give your wife plenty of reassuring touch. The right type of touch will make your wife feel comforted and safe, without you having to say a word. Hold her hand or put your arm around her in public, mindlessly rub her back, or take her feet onto your lap while watching TV (if she likes her feet rubbed). Any lull in conversation or activity is a good time for you to reassure her with touch. If she seems to misunderstand your motives at first, hang in there and keep

---

trying.

6) Give your wife lots of eye contact. This is a skill that seems to become less common between couples the longer they are married. Pay attention: Do you look at your wife when you speak to her, and when she speaks to you? You would never hold a business meeting without looking the other person in the eye; give your wife the same show of respect from now until death do you part.

7) Take the time to notice how beautiful your wife is while she is carrying your child, and tell her when you think so. Do this regularly, and with no motive other than to just let her know that you think she is gorgeous. Women need to hear this constantly, and pregnant women need to hear it even more. The only person in the world your wife really longs to hear it from is you. What a simple gift for you to give, and it doesn't cost a thing.

8) Speaking of gifts, many men don't know that it has become somewhat customary for husbands to give their wife a gift at the baby shower, and/or after the baby has been born. A good idea for a bridal shower gift would be a prenatal massage or pedicure, and a good gift for after the baby is born would be a small piece of jewelry or some kind of keepsake. Start looking now, and you're bound to find a good deal on something she will love. You'll come out looking like the best husband ever.

9) Be willing to talk to her about the topics she is concerned about. If she approaches you at the wrong time, such as in the middle of a football game or after a long day at work, take a moment to look at her and gently arrange a better time. Follow through by initiating the conversation when the time is right. You will find that conversations go much more smoothly when you are giving her your full attention.

10) Time in the word, alone and together. Yes, I'm repeating this! Nothing—I repeat, nothing—that you do, say, think, or feel apart from the Lord is going to meet your needs or your wife's needs. If your efforts are being misunderstood, unnoticed, or having any sort of negative effect, pray. The Lord has you, your wife, your child, your marriage, and everything good He has written for you, in His hands. Trust in Him to make you the husband your wife needs and the father your child will need. You are going to be an excellent dad!

"Do not be anxious about anything, but in every situation, by prayer and petition, with thanksgiving, present your requests to God." Philippians 4:6

I remember the first time Austin and I *really* prayed together. We had been married for years at that point, and we had been through much more than I've told you about so far. Our marriage was in a sad state, and we had decided to seek marital counseling. We had been instructed by our counselor to start praying together each night. So that night as we lay in bed, we tried it. It was awkward.

I was still new to my faith and prayer was still a pretty private venture for me. When it came to praying out loud in front of someone else, I found I didn't even know what to say. I felt embarrassed and inept. As my husband dutifully led us through our first prayer together, I remember how relieved and grateful I was to be able to follow his lead. I also remember how deeply it moved me to hear him asking God to watch over us. I didn't mind at all that it was a little clunky.

Whether you and your wife are seasoned Christians or not, praying together can feel awkward if you aren't already used to doing so. If you winced a little at the thought of leading your wife in prayer, don't be ashamed. Instead, I have an idea for you: Pray about it. That's right. Ask God to help you pray. Do not allow for years of hardship to force you into it like we did. Seek God's hand together now, so that you can raise your children to seek God's hand when they are grown.

• Do you and your wife pray together? If not, ask God to give you the courage to start. If so, ask God to continue to develop you and your wife into a family who prays together.

- **Homework: Read through the following guided prayer by yourself each day this week.**

"Dear Lord, thank You for being the true Head of my household. Thank You for being the One I can trust and count on as I try to provide and care for my family. Please help me to always remember that I am not alone. Thank You for providing financial principles for us to follow. Please help us to get our finances in order, and protect our marriage from the detrimental effects of financial difficulty. Please help my wife as she struggles in her new role and please help me to treat her as I would want to be treated. Help me remember to try the actions on the list of how to care for her, and help her to receive them. Lord, please give me the courage to initiate praying with her. Help us to become a family who prays together. In Jesus' name, amen."

WEEK 1

(*For Her*)

BUILDING YOUR HOUSEHOLD

"For you created my inmost being; you knit me together in my mother's womb. I praise you because I am fearfully and wonderfully made; your works are wonderful, I know that full well." Psalm 139:13-14

Isn't pregnancy amazing? I cannot even fathom the way that somehow our bodies just know how to grow new life inside of us. What an amazing testimony of God's unmatched intelligence and power, that He created our bodies with the ability to knit life together in such a way! He could just "snap" each of us into existence, but instead He allows our bodies to do it (as a result of the most intimate of acts, no less).

To be the vessel of such a miracle was, for me, so incredibly humbling. In fact, it was when I was pregnant with my first child that I found my way back to God after years of wandering around aimlessly without Him. The love I felt for this child, whom I had not yet met, illustrated so clearly the way God felt about me.

As I thought about my little boy, I knew I would love him through every mistake he would ever make. And it became so clear to me that God never stopped loving me through all of mine. As all my hopes and fears for my child were at the forefront of my thoughts, it was as if God really wanted me to hear Him saying, "You're my child, too!"

• **Read Psalm 139:13-16. Spend a moment on the fact that you, too, were knit together. Think about how you were known and loved before you were born. Do you see that God is saying to you, "You're my child, too"?**

• **Sit with the reality of how deeply you are loved. Thank God for giving up His only son because of His love for you.**

"The wise woman builds her house, but with her own hands the foolish one tears hers down." Proverbs 14:1

As we think about the miracle of life and you await the arrival of your own warm, wiggly, precious baby, I have a question for you: Where do husbands fit into the picture? While we women are wrapped up in the overwhelming flood of emotions that come from growing a newly created little being inside our body, what is our husband likely feeling?

Here's one possible answer: LEFT OUT. If you, the mom, are feeling closer to God, it's because you are supposed to. Don't shy away from it. But what about your husband? His body doesn't feel any different (unless he's joined you in indulging pregnancy cravings and put on some sympathy weight). He will never know what the little flutters are like (or the giant, alien-like rollovers).

He is stuck experiencing your baby from the outside for the entire duration of the pregnancy. While you are spending this time getting to know your baby by being in constant physical contact, he is still waiting for the day they will meet. I remember my husband saying he felt like his job was done once the baby was conceived— not because he wasn't interested or didn't care, but because there was just nothing more he felt he could do. It was easy for both of us to make the pregnancy either all about me or all about the baby.

You've probably been receiving a lot of input that this time is *all about you.* You need to take care of yourself. Your husband is there to cater to your every whim and drive out in the middle of the night to retrieve your late-night cravings. You are to rest, avoid anything that could be harmful to you and the baby, pamper yourself and indulge yourself in whatever ways necessary to make pregnancy more pleasant.

• **Going back to our previous discussion about what kind of Christ-centered family you want to be, what might be wrong with the idea of letting the pregnancy be "all about you" or "all about the baby"?**

"But I want you to realize that the head of every man is Christ, the head of a wife is her husband, and the head of Christ is God." 1 Corinthians 11:3

There's nothing wrong with taking care of yourself and your baby during pregnancy. But can you find anywhere in the Bible where it says that being pregnant lets you off the hook from "considering others better than yourself" (Philippians 2:3)? Likewise, does Scripture say once you are pregnant you can forget about your spouse and focus solely on Baby?

The truth is, everything about your baby, and the amazing miracle it is, should point you directly back to God. He is the one who is *really* growing your baby. You are so blessed to be able to experience it, but He is the one who deserves the glory!

• **Ask God to show you if you have allowed yourself or the baby to be elevated to too high of a status in your mind. Pray for Him to help you to place the members of your family in their appropriate roles in your household.**

• **Based on 1 Corinthians 11:3, what is the structure of a Christ-centered family?**

• **Be honest: How do you feel about your place in the household?**

"But the fruit of the Spirit is love, joy, peace, patience, kindness, goodness, faithfulness, gentleness, and self-control." Galatians 5:22-23

Going back to how I found my way back to God during my first pregnancy, I can assure you that learning God's plan for family structure was a tough pill for me to swallow. Before I met my husband I thought of myself as an independent, successful woman. (Believe me, I started young in that mindset all on my own. My mother, in observation of my expensive tastes when I was a little girl, informed me that I should marry a rich man. My response? That I intended to earn everything I would ever want, all by myself! She *loves* telling that story.)

Over time, as I have grown in my relationship with Christ, He has helped me to see that submission in marriage isn't quite what I understood it to be in my youth. I've come to understand that it doesn't have to equal total monetary dependence, nor does it mean a complete lack of personal identity or value of opinion. It's okay for me to utilize my God-given talents, both for fun and to earn an income. I own my own business, for goodness sake, and my husband encourages me to do so! But I do value, and seek, my husband's input in all of my decisions. And because of my willingness to submit my questions and ideas to him, there have been times when his logic and/or experience has saved me from making rash or emotional decisions, both in my business and personal life.

It has been nearly a decade since the day I met my husband. If you were to ask him how I have changed over the years, he would tell you that I am more loving, more joyful, less argumentative, kinder, more gentle, and more thoughtful in my speech—not just toward him, but toward everybody. These changes, along with my views on submission, could only be brought about by one thing: the Holy Spirit.

Where I didn't trust my husband before to be the head of our household, I have learned that I actually feel much safer when he is. When I defer to his natural leadership for making decisions, I find that we make decisions *together* more easily. Allowing him to take his God-given leadership role not only helps with decision-making, but also helps us avoid and resolve arguments.

Yes, there have been times when I've had to decide that I want to be married more than I want to be right. This has happened with both business and personal matters. I don't always want to give in. I like to win, and I like to be right. But in the times when I chose to swallow my pride and stop arguing, I found that my husband softened toward me in return and we were able to reach a compromise much more quickly.

God calls husbands and wives to submit to each other (Eph. 5:21). When you allow God to fill your marriage with the fruit of the Spirit, you will find that submitting to your husband is not so different from just treating him the way you would like to be treated.

• **Ask God to show you where there is imbalance in your relationship with your husband. Ask Him to fill your marriage with the fruits of the Spirit and to help you treat your husband as you would want to be treated.**

• **Which areas of your relationship do you think you struggle with the most when it comes to submitting to your husband? Be honest. Ask God to change your heart where it is appropriate.**

"And the second [commandment] is like it: 'Love your neighbor as yourself.' " Matthew 22:39

Earlier, I mentioned how difficult it is for husbands to feel included in pregnancy. I then went on to discuss the importance of proper roles in the family. I hope you are able to see now that by helping your husband to step into his role as leader of the family, you are including him in your pregnancy in the best possible way. You are freeing him to view the pregnancy not as an outsider but as the leader of something amazing. While I can't promise you that welcoming him as leader of the family will make him more interested in the less-important details of pregnancy (such as which color to paint the nursery), I can assure you that by aligning your household roles appropriately, you are more likely to feel like you are experiencing the miracle of your child *together*.

• **In what areas would you like to see your husband to "step up"? Ask God to give him courage to do so, and to give you the right words to encourage him—along with the wisdom to know when not to say anything at all.**

"Anyone who does not provide for their relatives, and especially for their own household, has denied the faith and is worse than an unbeliever." 1 Timothy 5:8

It is important for us as wives to understand that it can be just as hard for our husband to step into his new role as it is for us to step into ours. For one thing, the man of the house carries a great burden. Ingrained in men since the Garden of Eden is the knowledge that they will have to work hard for their food. While some men feel strongly motivated by this calling to provide and are outwardly driven to make it happen, others can feel reluctant to accept such a heavy responsibility. This inward resistance can have many causes, including fear of failure or apprehension toward change.

Chances are, whether your husband is outwardly driven or inwardly resistant, he is probably thinking about what the baby is going to cost. He is probably feeling the added pressure of providing for three (or more!). Regardless of who the main breadwinner is in your family, finances are likely to be a tricky topic during this time of change. It will be important that you are sensitive to your husband's feelings about money and provision.

It will also be important that you work together to get your finances in order. After finding that we were running out of money every month, and growing tired of arguing about it, we decided to adopt the financial principles taught in the Biblical finance classes which are offered at many larger churches. Once we had our budget set, and were in agreement about our financial plans, we found that arguing about money became a thing of the past. It was one of the best decisions we've ever made for our marriage.

• **How does your husband respond to his calling to provide for his family? Is he outwardly driven, or inwardly resistant? Ask God to soften your heart and help you understand where your husband is coming from on this sensitive topic.**

• Ask God to bless your conversations with your husband about finances. Ask Him to help you to get your finances in order and to seek Biblical financial advice if necessary.

• Ask God to bless the work of your husband's hands so that he can provide well for you regardless of your own income-earning potential.

• **Homework: Read through the following prayer each day this week.**

"Dear Lord, thank You so much for blessing my body with the ability to grow this little miracle. Thank You for creating me with the same love and attention You are giving to my child, and thank You for giving up Your own Child, for us. If I have elevated myself or this baby above where I should, please reveal that to me, and give me a balanced view of my own role in my household. Please help me to understand my husband's point of view with the topic of finances, and help me to be sensitive and encouraging with how I speak to him about them. Bless our conversations about money, and bless the work of his hands. Thank You, Lord, for the life You have given me and for the work I know You will do. In Jesus' name, amen."

WEEK 2

(For Us)

WHO STANDS WHERE?

• What did God show you this week about the structure of your home? Share any new insights with your spouse.

• Did God show you anything new about treating your spouse as you would like to be treated?

• Take a moment to pray and ask God to continue to work on your hearts and minds as you move forward with the devotional.

Hopefully in the last week, you and your spouse have spent some time allowing God to align your views on the correct structure of your household. I truly believe that if the only thing you take from this book is the agreement to keep Christ at the Head of your household, then it will be worth it. Even if you only had time to pray together once this week, consider it progress and continue to build your family together under God.

"Plans fail for lack of counsel, but with many advisers they succeed." Proverbs 15:22

During this time of change, as you prepare for your new roles as parents and work to have everything ready for the arrival of your baby, chances are you'll probably catch a few snags along the way. Even with the best of intentions between you and your spouse, you are bound to experience moments of tension. You will probably need some additional help.

When I went into labor with my son, our plan was for my husband to be my main supporter. My mom was there to oversee his caring for me. The idea was for her to use her experience to anticipate what I would need, and to pick up any slack where my husband left off. It sounded fool-proof.

My husband had been coaching me by himself for several hours by the time I was admitted to the hospital. When my mom arrived, excited and eager to help, he was ready for a break. He was hungry, as well as physically and emotionally tired from supporting me as long as he had. He stepped out into the waiting room to rest and gain support from his parents while my mom stayed to support me.

As soon as he left the room, I fell apart. I felt abandoned and alone, two emotions that sent me into a downward spiral of fear. Even though I had my mom there, I couldn't seem to refocus my attention enough to receive the help she wanted to offer. What was she supposed to do if I wasn't willing to accept her support?

Every couple of hours or so, my husband would need to step out again. Bathroom breaks, food, and the need for encouragement were all very legitimate reasons for him to go. Every time he re-entered the room, he came with renewed strength for supporting me. But because I was depending so heavily upon him, he would also return to find me in a more heightened state of need than before he left. None of us knew what to do.

I know you are probably hearing horror stories from nearly everyone you encounter right now, so I am going to fast-forward to the end and tell you that my son was indeed born later on—pink and healthy and beautiful. We even went on to have another child a few years later. The point isn't to scare you with my birth story. Truly, everything worked out in the end. The point of my story is to show you how imperative a good support team is for you. And not just during labor, but in the time leading up to it as well.

• **Besides each other, whom do you count on for support and guidance in life?**

"The way of fools seem right to them, but the wise listen to advice." Proverbs 12:15

If you are at all like we were, you may find that you don't have a lot of outside support during your pregnancy. My husband and I did not have our family structured with God as our Head, so we weren't looking to Him. We were the first of our friends to be having a baby so we couldn't look to them. And we could have spoken with our parents or families, but for the most part we didn't seek their support, either. It wasn't that we didn't recognize their wisdom and experience, but I suppose we were either too naïve or too proud to ask for it. That pretty much left us to figure out how to survive pregnancy on our own.

• **Make a list of possible outcomes that could come from not seeking support for your marriage during pregnancy, or from seeking support from the wrong people.**

• **Ask God to protect your family from these outcomes by giving you the wisdom to seek support from the right people.**

As you and your spouse talk today about who you want your support team to include, there are a few things you might want to consider:

1) **Is their family Christ-centered?** The best way to tell what someone really believes is to look at how they live. Who is Jesus to them, and what is His role in their home? Make sure you choose people who will affirm your roles as man and woman of the house and who will encourage you to keep Christ as the Head of your household.

2) **Have they had a positive experience with pregnancy and childbirth?** As new and different as pregnancy seems, you are not the first couple to go through it. Finding another couple who has experienced pregnancy and childbirth is a great way to help you realize how normal you and your spouse probably are. Plus, someone who had a positive experience is likely to have encouragement to offer, along with helpful advice for keeping your experience positive.

3) **Will they support both of you equally?** Sometimes during pregnancy, it can be difficult to tell whether a problem between you and your spouse is real, or if the issue at hand is being blown out of proportion by hormones. If you decide to vent to someone who feels an allegiance to you over your spouse, you might run the risk of them 'adding fuel to the fire' instead of helping to diffuse it. You will need to agree on supporters both of you can trust to defend your relationship. And, you will both need to commit to seeking these people out over those who will take sides, especially when you are angry or upset.

One last thing to consider as you think about who you want your support team to be during pregnancy is that you don't just have to choose from friends and family. Some people prefer to ask friends and family to support them through prayer, then seek outside support from pastors, mentors, small group leaders, or doulas. If you decide to seek outside support, make sure to ask questions in your interviews to ensure that they meet all of the above criteria.

• **For today's closing activity, spend a few minutes with your spouse thinking about the people in your life and assigning them to either your Prayer Team or your Support Team. (Remember, you should both agree that the people on your Support Team meet all of the above-listed criteria. If you can't seem to agree on where a person belongs, place them on your Prayer Team.)**

Prayer Team:

Support Team:

Once you have agreed as a couple about who you will trust for advice, guidance, and prayer throughout your pregnancy and childbirth experience, you will need to ask these people to commit to being there for you. Be sure to outline what you need from them, thoroughly explaining the parameters of the support you are requesting from them. It will be up to them to decide whether they feel capable of meeting your needs.

• **Homework: Pray the following prayer together each day this week.**

"Father, please show us which people You want us to look to and lean on for advice and guidance. Whether we are having issues in our marriage, seeking support during childbirth, or looking to learn as parents, we ask that You help us to know who to speak to. If we have problems deciding, please help the right people to emerge, and make it clear to us so that it won't be a source of contention between us. Once we have decided, please help us to remain committed to seeking support from these people, even when we are angry. In Jesus' name, amen."

WEEK 2

(For Him)

TO EVERYTHING THERE IS A SEASON

"In this same way, husbands ought to love their wives as their own bodies. He who loves his wife loves himself." Ephesians 5:28

The fact that you are working through this devotional with your wife tells me that you are a loving husband. I realize that for many of you, it was probably your wife's idea and you are being kind enough to go along with it. I hope that by now you can see that this devotional truly is for both of you. There are definitely two sides to pregnancy. It can be hard on fathers, too.

I have been told that one of the most difficult things about pregnancy for men is the topic of sex. Because most couples tend to fall into a groove during marriage that often gets disrupted by pregnancy, many men are left wondering how long it will be until things get back to "normal." Some men feel left out or forgotten as their wives' thoughts become engrossed in pregnancy, childbirth, and preparing for a baby.

It's Austin again. There is one thing I always share with my buddies when they find out their wife is pregnant. I always say, 'Hang in there. You will get your wife back.'

Sometimes my husband is willing to say what other people will only think. But I have to give him credit. At least he is honest. Perhaps you looked at what he had to say and you don't relate at all—your wife is much the same pregnant as she was before. If that is the case, then good for you. But stay with me anyway. Perhaps there is something you'll be able to share that will help others, or, maybe you'll still learn a thing or two about what your wife needs from you right now.

• **Ask God to prepare your heart to learn about the season of pregnancy.**

"There is a time for everything, and a season for every activity under the heavens." Ecclesiastes 3:1

For many men, pregnancy can make things seem...different. If you can relate even a little, it might help to remember that this is just a season. The first thing you should probably know about this season is how long it lasts.

It is good to be aware that your baby's birthday does not mark the end of this season. The first 12 weeks of your baby's life are commonly referred to as the "fourth trimester," because having a new baby in the house is an adjustment period of its own. So as you count down the days to your baby's due date, know that it will be a few months longer before your family starts to find its "new normal." But be encouraged: You *will* get your wife back.

• **Take a minute to think about the timeline you have in mind surrounding the birth of your child and your life returning to "normal." Ask God to reveal to you if you are being unrealistic.**

• **Ask God to give you an understanding of the amazing changes taking place in your wife, and ask Him to give you realistic expectations about your relationship during this time.**

Let's take a quick look at what is happening in your wife's body during each of the four trimesters:

First trimester.

When it comes to sex during the first trimester, you might find your wife just doesn't feel up for it. This might make sense to you if your wife is feeling sick from pregnancy hormones. But even if she isn't sick, her hormones are still at work in new ways that are beyond her control. This may affect her sex drive.

If your wife's sex drive is reduced (or gone), try not to take it personally. Remember that pressuring her or making her feel guilty will only damage your relationship. Be encouraged with the knowledge that your body will also adjust to the changes; in time your hormones will balance out, making any decrease in sexual activity more bearable.

In the meantime, whether your sex life has been affected or not, try to see your wife as God sees her. Keep in mind that she *wants* to feel normal, and show that you care by offering your kindness. If she's not feeling up for sex, she may appreciate other forms of touch, such as hugs and cuddling. Know that sometimes, she might just need to cry. There is nothing you need to do but hold her and tell her everything will be fine. (We women really love to hear that.) Remind her that while she is the one carrying the baby, both of you are expecting.

Second trimester.

This trimester is also known as the "honeymoon" phase of pregnancy. While marital intimacy is about much more than just a physical urge, it is possible that your wife might be more open to the idea now than she was in the first trimester.

Like we discussed in the "Notes For Dad" section, it will help if you are the one to take the initiative in finding ways to spend time together. Schedule dates with her. You don't have to spend a lot of money; the idea is to just enjoy spending time with her. This is the most normal your wife will probably feel for the next six months. Help her enjoy it.

Tip from Austin: Keep your motives in check when you take your wife on a date. She's likely to be turned off by an ulterior motive for sex, but if you just focus on enjoying her company, sex can sometimes be a natural result.

Third Trimester.

Your childbirth class is likely to mention that sex is a good method for naturally inducing labor, and there will probably come a time when your wife is willing to try anything to get the baby to come. This is an aspect of pregnancy many men are thankful for.

Prostaglandins (produced by men) help soften the cervix so that it can dilate, and Oxytocin (produced by women) is responsible for causing contractions. So, not only is mutual sexual fulfillment a meaningful way of connecting and expressing your love for each other, but it is also God's way of helping labor to start in an enjoyable way.

Sometimes, women don't want to have sex at this point because they are fearful of going into labor. If this is the case with your wife, the best thing you can do is pray with her. Try to help her remember that fear is not from God (2 Timothy 1:7), and help her to ask for God to give her peace. The more you listen to her concerns and join her in trying to overcome them, the better she is likely to feel.

The "Fourth Trimester."

The first 12 weeks of your baby's life will be an adjustment period for everyone. During the first six weeks after your baby is born, your wife's body will have some healing to do. Doctors generally recommend waiting until around six weeks postpartum before resuming sexual activity.

At that six-week mark, it is important to keep in mind that just because the doctor says your wife is physically ready to resume having sex, that doesn't necessarily mean she will be emotionally or mentally ready to do so. If she needs more time, don't take it personally. Her hormones may just need a little longer to even out, or maybe she's just feeling a little insecure about her baby weight. Or, perhaps she is honestly exhausted from caring for the baby. Just keep doing the things you learned during the other trimesters, and have faith that in time things will eventually return to normal.

• **Ask God to give you patience and to help you focus on being the supportive husband your wife deserves.**

In addition to the ways you have shown your love and support during the first three trimesters (such as non-sexual touch, spending time together, and praying with her), you can also help her to feel loved just by helping her out with the house and baby. She deserves a break. Bring home dinner, or be open to having sandwiches or cereal. If she is tired of being cooped up in the house and feels like going out, maybe a trip to a restaurant is in order.

Remember, this is not forever. You're nearing the end of this season. Be forgiving, be patient, and be helpful. The house doesn't have to look perfect, but you will both feel better if it is at least picked up. Maybe you could help with this. For now, just try to focus on being a team player. Remember to thank your wife for taking care of your child. And she will be thankful for your help, too.

• **Ask God to bring balance to your sexual relationship, and to help your marital bond to strengthen during the pregnancy and postpartum periods.**

"No temptation has overtaken you except what is common to us all. God is faithful; he will not let you be tempted beyond what you can bear. But when you are tempted, he will also provide a way out so that you can endure it." 1 Corinthians 10:13

I'll never forget the time when a business acquaintance of Austin's (who was not morally upstanding) emailed him a purposely mislabeled link to a photo of a scantily-clad woman. I was pregnant at the time, and I can't even describe how upset and hurt I was when I came across the photo on our computer. Even though it wasn't even Austin's fault, I was furious at him. Then, after I found it in my heart to forgive him, I got really insecure. With my round belly and expanding limbs, I definitely *did not* look like that supermodel. It was a really hard time for me to get through.

If this is how I felt because of an innocent mistake on my husband's part, I can only imagine how women feel whose husbands *do* purposely look at other women. Especially during the pregnancy and postpartum period, it will be important for your wife to know that you only have eyes for her. This means when she's there with you, as well as when she isn't. As the loving and committed husband that you are, pray continually for God to give you a pure heart and the strength to act accordingly.

• **Read Psalm 51:10 as a prayer.**

Lastly, nobody's sex life is perfect, especially during pregnancy and immediately postpartum. But for some couples, there are more deep-rooted problems that can stem from before they even knew each other. If you feel that you are experiencing issues which go beyond the parameters discussed here, seek counseling. If at all possible, go before your baby comes. You don't want to inadvertently pass any strongholds on to your children (2 Corinthians 10:4). Also, keep in mind that you don't have to have experienced a so-called "trauma" in order to benefit from counseling. Often times, if a problem keeps popping up—even if it seems minor—it probably takes root somewhere in the past, and a good counselor can help fix it.

Good counselors don't take sides. The best way you can help yours to stay unbiased is to participate in counseling with your wife.
-Austin

• **Ask God to help you to love your wife in the way she needs to be loved, and ask Him to help you to be the husband and father He wants you to be.**

• **Homework: Pray the following prayer each day this week, on your own.**

"Dear Lord, thank You for the insight you have given me about my wife's experience with pregnancy. Please help me to love her without motive and to continually give myself up for her the way You did for me. I ask You to give me a balanced view of our relationship, and to bless our sex life. I ask You to deliver me from the temptation of impure thoughts and deeds, and guide us in seeking counseling if it will make our marriage stronger. Thank You for being my source of strength in this time. In Jesus' name, amen."

WEEK 2

(For Her)

BIRTH PLAN...OR IDOL?

• When you think about your child, what do you want them to know about you the most?

• In what ways do you plan to make this known to them?

As I mentioned before, I was just starting to get to know God again when I was pregnant with my son. It always strikes me as particularly amazing how of all the attributes He could have chosen to reveal to me about Himself during that time (such as His power, His majesty, or His sovereignty, just to name a few), the first thing He wanted me to know about Him was that He loved me. *He* loved *me*. How can the Almighty God be so humble?

Then again, when I think about my own son, that is exactly what I want him to know about me. More than anything else, I just want him to know I love him.

So far in this book, we have spent a lot of time discussing the kind of Christ-centered family you want to have and your role as the woman of that family. Keeping Christ at the head of your home and allowing Him to be the One in control is of great importance. And as you seek to do that, you will probably be thinking ahead to how you can be the best parent possible.

For me, this began with the choices I made surrounding my baby's health during pregnancy. I exercised and rested appropriately, ate well and avoided unhealthy substances. But I still wanted to do more. In what other ways could I give my child my very best?

I started talking to other women about their own childbirth experiences. To tell you the truth, most of the stories I heard were a little frightening. I heard about long labors, pain, fearful emotions, and in some cases, emergency caesarian births. Haunted by the feelings of fear and lack of control that their stories caused me, I felt determined to make sure that none of their scary stories would happen to me—or my child. I started putting together my birth plan.

• **How have other people's stories affected your view of childbirth?**

• **Ask God to remove any fear that others may have inadvertently caused you. Ask Him to replace that fear with a balanced view of childbirth that you can apply to each story you hear in the future.**

Perhaps you haven't put much thought into having a birth plan, or aren't familiar with the term. A birth plan is a way for expectant parents to look at all of their options for childbirth and decide ahead of time which of those options are best for them. I began learning about my options with online research.

Through my research, I learned that childbirth, and how you go about it, is a hot topic. There are a lot of strong opinions surrounding childbirth that I hadn't been aware of. It seemed like whether I was reading about un-medicated home births or elective cesareans in a hospital, somebody had an opinion with statistics to back it up about why it was the better choice. The one underlying message that I continued to pick up on, however, was that the way my baby was born was extremely important, as if it would somehow determine everything else about his life.

If I wanted my baby to be happy and healthy, I would need to do everything just "right"—and it was up to me to decide what "right" was. If I chose the wrong option, or even worse, wasn't able to perform according to the birth plan I designed, there were negative outcomes that my child could face. In wanting to do what was best for my child, my birth plan and my ability to stick to it became very much a measure of my own worth. I cared a lot about proving to myself (and to others) that I was a good mother, and my performance during childbirth was going to be my first chance to do so. Before my child was even born, I wanted everyone to think I was Supermom.

• **When it comes to your childbirth experience, what does "giving your child the very best" mean to you? What would this effort entail?**

In addition to measuring my worth as a mother, my birth plan became very much about proving my worth as a woman. Among certain groups, the belief is that as women we are entitled to experience natural childbirth, and any other means of birth would equal a "lesser" experience. These people reason that if anything should happen to derail our birth plan, we should feel as if we have been robbed of something we deserve.

Since then I have come to see that their mindset is perhaps overly biased. We are blessed to live in a time and place where medical interventions are available, and besides that, women who have epidurals and/or give birth via c-section are still *giving birth*. At the time, however, I believed what they said. I worried about whether I would be able to "make it" through natural childbirth. I started to feel afraid, as if accepting the medical interventions available to me would somehow be an indication of my failure.

I also read many articles by women who seemed to think that their doctors were only in it for the money, and that any intervention their doctor suggested should be treated with suspicion. Extreme as these ideas may seem, I bought into them as well. I planned to resist every option my doctor presented me, because in addition to a fear of failure, I also entered childbirth with a distrust in my doctor's motives.

My birth plan became about proving my worth and ability as a woman, and I was not going to let anyone take it from me. My birth plan was supposed to make me feel educated, prepared, and supported. Sadly, however, I became suspicious, defensive, and afraid.

"Therefore, my dear friends, flee from idolatry." 1 Corinthians 10:14

As a doula, I am a huge proponent of having a birth plan. It is important that you are informed on your options prior to going into labor, because once you are in the delivery room you might not have the time or presence of mind to make very many decisions.

However, as my story illustrates, it is possible to go too far. Your birth plan can become a measure of your worth, or even become like an idol that you trust instead of God. When you give your birth plan a heightened measure of importance, it can become a source of fear. If you feel pressure to perform a certain way during childbirth, I urge you to remember that your worth comes from God alone. He loves you for exactly who you are and there is nothing you have to prove. Nothing about the way your child is born is an indication of your worth as a mother, a woman, or a person. If you have a hard time comprehending that, think about your own child and how unconditionally you value him or her. That's how God feels about you.

Perhaps you realized as I shared my story that I was taking my birth plan too seriously, but, at the time, I didn't realize it. If you had asked me then, I would have assured you that my motives were pure and that I just wanted to do what was best for my baby. And yet, look how I was filled with fear and how it became about proving my worth. See how it consumed me and changed the focus of my birth plan from being about God's miracle to instead being about my performance. I can just imagine how that "roaring lion" must have been prowling around me, encouraging the lies I believed about the source of my worth and filling me with fear (1 Peter 5:8).

• **Take a moment to sit quietly and observe your thoughts surrounding the birth of your child. Ask God to help you see what is really going on in your heart and in your mind.**

"I will instruct you and teach you in the way you should go; I will counsel you with my loving eye on you." Psalm 32:8

As you research your options and decide what is important to you, I have a recommendation: Pray about it. You are going to need a strong sense of discernment as you seek other people's opinions about what should be important to you. If you submit yourself to God's will, then you can trust in His wisdom as you consider your options. You don't need to be afraid as you create your birth plan because you don't have to figure out what you should include all by yourself. You have God on your side.

• **Ask God to come alongside you as you plan for the birth of your child. Ask for His protection, His wisdom, and His guidance. Ask Him to give you discernment so that you can achieve a balanced view of your birth options.**

"Instead, you ought to say, 'If it is the Lord's will, we will live and do this or that.' " James 4:15

Having a birth plan in place will be helpful for making decisions once you are in labor. Remember, however, that God already knows what your labor will really look like. Just as He knows the number of hairs on your head (Luke 12:7), He also knows how many contractions you will have before your baby comes. Plan as you may for the birth of your child, He is the One in control. Isn't that great? It's not all up to you; it's up to the One who created the stars, the heavens, the entire earth and everything in it—including you. You need to be willing to accept the fact that your real birth story may look vastly different from the one you have planned. But you can trust God to know what He is doing.

• **Try this: The next time someone asks you about your birth plan, begin your answer by including the phrase from James 4:15, "If it is the Lord's will, then..." See how it changes the way you feel about your birth plan.**

• **Homework: Spend the next couple of days praying the following prayer.**

"Father, thank You for reminding me that my worth comes from You alone. If I am overly concerned about choosing the right birth options, or if my motives are different that what I think they are, please reveal that to me. Please give me a balanced view of my birth plan and give me discernment as I choose what is best for my child. Thank You for being the One who is really in control of what my labor will look like. Help me to trust You. In Jesus' name, amen."

WEEK 2, DAY 2

(For Her)

SEX AND CANDY

"The wife does not have authority over her own body but yields it to her husband. In the same way, the husband does not have authority over his own body but yields it to his wife." 1 Corinthians 7:4

I don't know about you, but I love chocolate. In fact, there are days when I feel like I *need* it. I usually keep a private stash in my refrigerator, hidden from my children, so that if I want some I can have it—without having to share. The other day, I was having one of those days. Something whispered the word, "chocolate," and I could just taste the velvety goodness in my mouth. In anticipation of the delicious satisfaction a little piece would bring, I opened up the refrigerator and looked inside, only to find that it held no chocolate whatsoever. I chided myself for forgetting to pick more up at the store, and then proceeded to eat practically everything else in the house. Nothing would satisfy the craving. As I added the calories in my head and tried to reason that I did not need anything more to eat, I thought to myself, "Oh, well...I still have to have chocolate."

That afternoon after picking my son up from school, we went to the grocery store. In his presence and right before his little eyes, I bought chocolate. Yes, I was so desperate for chocolate that I was even willing to share.

I heard something recently that brought a whole new light to my love affair with chocolate. It was proposed that the chemical compounds that are released in a woman's brain after consuming chocolate are similar to those released after having sex. While I have heard before about how men physically need sex, I have never been able to comprehend exactly what that meant—until now. When I think about what that *need* for chocolate feels like, it helps me to understand what a man's need for sex might feel like. When I need my chocolate, there is nothing I can do about it except to have some. And while consuming a little bit every now and then is nice, I would really love it if I could have a lot of it very frequently. (Sound like anyone you know?)

"Do not deprive each other except perhaps by mutual consent and for a time, so that you may devote yourselves to prayer. Then come together again so that Satan will not tempt you because of your lack of self-control. I say this as a concession, not a command." 1 Corinthians 7:5-6

Ladies, it is time for you to realize that chances are, you are what your husband craves most. Whether you are dressed glamorously for a party or in your maternity sweat pants, the desire that he feels for you is probably the same. If you are like me, this can be hard to understand sometimes—especially when you are tired from a long day of being pregnant. But I can imagine how I would have felt on that day that I needed chocolate if the store clerk had told me I wasn't allowed to buy any.

It's important to remember that just as you need your favorite treat (whatever it may be), your husband also needs his—and his favorite treat is most likely special time with you. Remember that he carries a lot of pressure as the man of the house. By sharing yourself with him you are helping him to escape for a while in a way that will bring him renewed perspective on life.

A friend of mine once told me about some great advice she had gained from a bridal shower: "Think of sex as a ministry." At times when you aren't "feeling it," she explained, remember that sex is important to your husband because God designed him that way. Sex is one way you can serve your husband and help him experience God's goodness in his life. In this way, fulfilling your husband's sexual needs is actually a calling!

• **Ask God to bless your marriage with a healthy sexual relationship with your husband. Ask Him to bring balance to this part of your relationship, softening each of your hearts to the needs of the other.**

"The weapons we fight with are not the weapons of the world. On the contrary, they have divine power to demolish strongholds." 2 Corinthians 10:4

For some couples, problems with sex go much deeper than just being "too tired." Just because you are married and expecting a child, does not necessarily mean that your sex life has ever been what you would consider "normal." If this applies to you, I want you to know that you are not alone.

As a doula, I have been trained with startling statistics

surrounding the high percentage of couples who feel abnormal in this area. For many men and women, these problems can stem from situations that occurred before their child was conceived. If you have a marital problem that keeps popping up again and again (it doesn't necessarily have to be a sexual problem), chances are it takes root in the times before you and your husband even met. It may have even been passed down from generation to generation within your family as a spiritual stronghold.

Although it may seem like now is not the right time to delve into difficult emotional issues, let me assure you that it is. Addressing these issues now will help you to avoid inadvertently passing your strongholds onto your children (2 Corinthians 10:2). Keep in mind that even people who have never experienced a so-called "trauma" can benefit from seeking counseling.

Most counselors find it helpful to the marriage if you seek counseling together first. If separate counseling is needed, it still helps for a good relationship between you, your spouse, and your counselor to already have been established. A good counselor will want to avoid inadvertently favoring one of you over the other, and will want to avoid sending the message that one of you is the "problem." Attending together will help the counselor to achieve these goals.

For those of you who don't have insurance or who have expensive co-pays, it might be helpful to know that many Christian counselors will work for discounted rates (or for free), or know of someone who does. Christian pregnancy centers can also be a good place to check. Be sure to do your research and find someone with good credentials and a good reputation. You might be surprised how quickly issues can be resolved with the help of a good counselor (and lots of prayer).

• **Ask God to show you if you would benefit from getting counseling before your child is born. Ask Him to give you the courage to seek out a counselor and to help you find the right one.**

• **Homework: Each day, pray the following prayer by yourself.**

"Dear Lord, please help me to be sensitive to my husband's need for sex. Help me to see that he desires special time with me because You made him that way, and help us to find a healthy balance in our sexual relationship. If we need additional help with difficult issues, give us courage and clear our paths so that we can find a good counselor. Thank You for what you have revealed to me today. In Jesus' name, amen."

WEEK 3

(For Us)

THE BIG DAY

• Take a minute to think about what God has shown you from the first two weeks of the devotional. Share with your spouse.

• Ask God to prepare your hearts to receive what He has for you in today's lesson.

Your baby's birthday: In the years to come, you will celebrate this day with pure joy as you remember the first time you held your child. If you have been to the birthday parties of other people's kids, maybe all you imagine is sugared-up little goofballs running around creating chaos. I can tell you right now, that is only the tiniest portion of the picture when you are celebrating your own child's birthday. Each year, right up there next to Christmas, your child's birthday is bound to provide some of your family's most treasured memories.

I could not even imagine the day my first child would be born. As I approached my due date, I kept having a recurring dream about going to the hospital. In the dream, although I was supposed to be in labor, I felt nothing. Then I would blink and my baby would already be in my arms. Confused, I would ask the nurse, "I already had him? But what was labor like?" I was so unable to imagine what labor would be like, I literally couldn't even dream of it.

Perhaps you're more imaginative than me. Perhaps you've had a descriptive friend or have read a lot, and you think you have an idea of what labor will be like. But until you've actually experienced it, it's still hard to know what to expect. And if you are like most couples, the numerous 'unknowns' that surround labor and childbirth probably contribute to some of your most pressing concerns.

"Be still and know that I am God..." Psalm 46:10

These are the birth stories of a couple of people I have been lucky enough to call clients (names were changed for privacy):

Story 1: 'Julie' had a completely normal pregnancy. She spent a lot of time praying and seeking a deeper relationship with the Lord as her baby grew. However, she was physically uncomfortable by the end of it, and felt ready for the baby to come. She started having contractions on a Sunday at about noon. They steadily became more frequent until she headed into the hospital around midnight. She and her husband prayed together before going to the hospital and again when they got there, asking God to send His Holy Spirit to be with them. They had scripture verses prepared to help renew Julie's spirit as she endured each contraction. Her labor progressed quickly, and their baby was born by 6am on Monday morning with no complications.

Story 2: 'Megan' also had a normal pregnancy, but because she was two weeks overdue, her doctor decided the baby should be induced. Before starting the induction process, Megan and her husband prayed for God's presence and peace of mind. A few short hours into the induction process, before she had even felt any contractions, the on-call doctor came in abruptly and recommended an immediate c-section. They were distraught by the sudden news, at first questioning the doctor's knowledge, and then his motives. They asked for privacy. Together, they prayed for wisdom and discernment.

A peace settled over them as they prayed, and both of their hearts changed from being adamantly opposed to the c-section, to knowing it was the right choice. Their baby boy was born healthy just 30 minutes later, by emergency c-section. They learned after the baby was delivered that he had been awkwardly positioned as well as wrapped numerous times in his umbilical cord—a combination that could have taken a heavy toll on the baby, had they decided to continue to labor. They praised God for changing their hearts with His blessed discernment. God had protected their child.

- **As different as these stories are, they have something in common. What is it?**

"Remain in me, as I also remain in you. No branch can bear fruit all by itself; it must remain in the vine. Neither can you bear fruit unless you remain in me." John 15:4

As you attend your childbirth classes you are likely to be told that the trick to enduring the demands of labor is to look deep within yourself and draw upon your inner strength. While I cannot deny that labor is physically and emotionally demanding for both parents, I cannot stress enough that *we* are not the source of our strength. God is. Childbirth is not a measure of ability or will. It is an experience to be shared with the One who created it; a time to share our difficulty with Him simply because we know He cares (1 Peter 5:7).

• **Ask God to be there with you on the day of your baby's birth. Ask Him to send His Holy Spirit and surround you with His presence in an unmistakable way.**

"They will call on me, and I will answer them; I will be with them in trouble, I will deliver them and honor them." Psalm 91:15

When you are asking for God's presence, His *relationship*, His answer will always be a resounding "Yes." He wants nothing more than to be there with you on the day of your child's birth (not to mention each day before and after). Consider the words in the verse above as if they are from God Himself, to you. You asked if He will come; He says He will. Consider it His divine RSVP. Yes, He'll be there for your baby's birth day.

• **Today's closing activity:** Spend a few minutes in observation of what your mind imagines when you think about what labor will be like for you (or your wife). What time of day is it? What are you doing? Is there music? How do you feel? Share your answers with your spouse. (There are no right or wrong answers; it's just fun to become aware of what you are each envisioning.) Then ask yourself: Where is God in this picture? Ask Him to give you a mental picture of where He will be. If you realize that you are envisioning a scenario that makes you feel negatively, ask God to give you a new mental picture on which to focus.

	What He Envisions	What She Envisions
Time of Day		
What are You Doing?		
Music?		
How Do You Feel?		
Other details?		
Where is God?		

• **Homework: Pray the following prayer together each day this week.**

"Father, thank You for Your assurance that You will be there for our child's birth. Please help us to remain in You like a branch remains in the vine. In Jesus' name, amen."

WEEK 3

(For Him)

HER COACH AND HER SAVIOR

"So do not fear, for I am with you; do not be dismayed, for I am your God. I will strengthen you and help you; I will uphold you with my righteous right hand." Isaiah 41:10

So far, out of all the couples I have worked with as a doula, I have never been contacted by a husband looking for support during childbirth. It's always the wife. Sometimes, the husbands have even seemed a little reluctant to invite a stranger into such an intimate occasion.

Truly, I can see where they are coming from. It doesn't take long, however, before the men I work with start to realize that I am there to help them be the man their wife needs.

As the man of the house and main childbirth coach, what you need to know is what to say/not say, and do/not do during labor. That's it. So, I'll cut to the chase and let you hear from my husband:

> **Austin here. When I was coaching Jen through labor, I just used the weight room mentality of "almost there...just one more...you've got this."**

Men! How you guys say things in so few words baffles me. But really, he's got it exactly right. Coaching your wife through labor can be roughly compared to coaching a buddy through a workout. She'll sweat. She'll grunt. She'll breathe hard. She'll probably complain and want it to be over with. If you've ever spent any time lifting weights in a gym, then this should be nothing new. Except this time you'll be coaching a woman, which means she might cry, too (but don't let that scare you; it's just a part of the process for some women).

You will need to be mentally present as you coach your wife through labor, just as you would be if you were spotting someone at the gym. Your job is to stay focused as you coach her through each contraction, observing and correcting her form, and encouraging her belief in her ability (and God's ability). Honestly, that's it. All you have to do is encourage her and be there to hold the barbell with her if she starts to lose her grip. Let's break this down a little more just to be sure you know what I mean.

• **Ask God to give you an understanding of your role as your wife's childbirth coach.**

Coaching her through contractions

Just like lifting a set of weights, each contraction will only last a certain amount of time, and it will take multiple sets in order for it to do any good. As labor progresses and your wife gets tired, the contractions will become more intense and difficult, but each will still only last for no more than a couple of minutes. Help her to focus only on the current contraction, instead of on the entire labor. Remind her that God knows how many contractions it will take to bring the baby. After completing a particularly difficult contraction, remind her that she is done forever with that one, and to rest. Congratulate her hard work often.

Observing and correcting her form

If you were with someone who had never lifted weights before, you would probably take extra care to remind them of correct form, positioning, and breathing. Same thing here. The correct form during labor requires that your wife release any tense muscles in her face, hands and feet, and body. She should change positions at least a couple of times per hour. And breathing should come through loose lips and a soft belly. These are all techniques you should learn in your childbirth class; your job is just to remind her of them during each contraction.

Encouraging her belief in her ability (and God's ability)

The most important thing you can be watching for as your wife's labor coach is what her thoughts and emotions are doing. She will probably oscillate between being completely mentally present, and completely mentally checked-out. The hormones in her body will take over, and each contraction will eventually need her full attention. Sometimes, either during or between contractions, a laboring mother can come to realize that she is not in control of her situation. It can be scary. As labor progresses and becomes more difficult, your wife is probably going to start feeling like she can't do it.

Your job is not to be her savior. Your job is to be her coach.

"I keep my eyes always on the Lord. With him at my right hand, I will not be shaken." Psalm 16:8

When she starts to lose her grip, start with the weight room mentality. Get her attention enough to correct her form, her breathing, and her positioning. Encouragement and praise during and after each contraction are imperative. Remind her that her body was created to do this. But remember, there's only so much you can do. At some point, you will also realize that you are not in control of the situation. Going with our weight room theme, here is an acronym to help you decide what to do next:

WEIGHTS

Wait. Don't become impatient. Remember that it will take time and that there's nowhere else you need to be. Remind your wife of the same.

Eat. It is very possible to confuse hunger with negative feelings about the birth situation. By this point in labor, if you are starting to feel negatively, it's probably time for you to make sure you are nourished and hydrated. Call a friend or family member to bring you something, and get your wife a popsicle or honey. Make sure both of you are drinking water.

Intercession. Pray over your wife, asking God to make His presence known. Ask for His peace and His protection to surround your wife and renew both of your spirits.

God. Think about how labor has gone so far, and look for God's hand. A great nurse, a timely exam, even a green light on the way to the hospital are all examples of ways God may have already shown His face. Look for Him. Tell your wife where you see Him. Remind her that He is there, and that He is in control.

Hands. There is a saying that goes, "Be where your hands are." Stop thinking about how much longer things will take, or about any of the

---

'what-ifs' that may be going through your minds. "Be where your hands are" means that you need to return fully to the present. One contraction at a time.

Touch. By always maintaining physical contact between you and your wife, you are communicating that you are both in it together. Neither of you are alone. This will be comforting to both of you. Your wife is likely to forget most of what labor is like, but she is not likely to forget your comforting touch. Be sure to use what you learn in your childbirth class.

Scripture. Your wife has a page full of scripture prepared for this day. Read one to her at a time, and encourage her to meditate on it during her next contraction. If you need to, you can even write it on the dry-erase board in her hospital room so that she can look at it during contractions. Remember that while it is hard for you to see her like this, you don't have to save her. Direct her to her true Savior.

• **Ask God to help you see Him during labor. Ask Him to give you the right words and actions to help your wife cope, and for patience and discernment as you support your wife. Thank Him for remaining with you during this time.**

"Be kind and compassionate to one another, forgiving each other, just as in Christ God forgave." Ephesians 4:32

After you have experienced labor and delivery together, God willing, you and your wife are going to be holding your baby. All the tension of your childbirth experience will melt away as you marvel at the little miracle in your arms. I want to encourage you to use this tender time to also check in with your wife about how she feels about her childbirth experience. There may have been moments of tension or even disappointment during labor, for which you may need to forgive each other.

• **Initiate a prayer with your wife, asking God to help you both to forgive each other so that you may enter parenthood as a united couple.**

Note from Austin: Remember that helping your wife through labor is a learning experience. The next time you coach her through labor, you'll have a better idea of what to do.

• **Homework: Read the following prayer by yourself each day this week.**

"Lord, please help me to remember the weight room mentality and WEIGHTS acronym. Please help me to see You when we are in labor so that I don't feel like I have to be my wife's Savior. Please help me to point her to You so that You can bring her the comfort she needs. Thank You, Lord, for my family.

Please protect us and guide us. In Jesus' name, amen."

WEEK 3

(For Her)

BIRTH STORIES ARE GOD STORIES

"If you remain in me and my words remain in you, ask whatever you wish and it will be given to you." John 15:7

• **Ask God to prepare your heart to receive His message for you today.**

As I settle in for a morning of writing at my old kitchen table, I am reminded that God knows what we need. I bought this table off of Craigslist a couple of years back. It was a pretty good deal; solid pine with an 18" leaf (*almost* big enough to fit the whole family at gatherings) and refinished in the cutest manner which happens to match our house décor perfectly.

One problem: the chairs feel like they're going to crumble to the ground when you sit on them. I didn't notice when I bought them, but these chairs have been reinforced in every possible way underneath, and they still wobble. No, not wobble. They *glide*. Every time we have guests, they look like they're afraid we're trying to trick them into being on America's Funniest Home Videos. Of course that wasn't the plan when we bought the set, but at the rate these chairs are going, and if we keep our cameras ready, we just might end up there. Unfortunately, financially speaking, getting a new table just isn't a priority for us right now. So, we've just had to take our chances.

Here's how I know God hears us. Without praying for a table (because honestly, we have more pressing concerns to pray about right now), right out of the blue, the parents of some friends of ours told us they'd like us to have their dining room set. This kind couple has never been to our house. They've never experienced the *glide*. Still, for whatever reason, they thought of us when trying to decide what to do with their *immaculate* oak set. Two leaves instead of one. Up to 10 seats instead of just 6. Perfectly clean, very comfortable, *sturdy* chairs. Just what I should have bought in the first place. Coincidence? I think not.

Now, this "nod from God," as I like to call it, could easily be explained away as random or lucky. Or, the credit could all be given to our generous donors. (Although, in their humility, they would never take it.) Explain it as you may, I am now convinced that what happened was nothing short of divine intervention. God saw our need, and He met it. Without my even having to ask. And truth be told, He wasn't just fulfilling my need for a table. He was fulfilling my need to hear from Him. In the midst of our family's many as-yet unanswered prayers, He sent me a message: "I see you. I love you. I've got you covered."

• **When have you received a "nod from God"? Ask God to help you see Him in your everyday coincidences.**

Your birth story is going to be a lot like that. You will have needs that you won't even know to ask for God to help with. But He knows. There will be things that could be easily explained away: a great nurse, a timely exam, even a green light on the way to the hospital. Through your childbirth experience, God desires to reveal more of Himself to you. What it will come down to is whether or not you are watching. You have already invited Him to be there on that day; now you're going to need to watch for His arrival.

• **Ask God to help you to see Him in your childbirth experience. Ask Him to reveal Himself in an unmistakable way to you and your husband.**

"How great is the goodness, which you have stored up for those who fear you, which you bestow in the sight of all on those who take refuge in you." Psalm 31:19

Going into labor for my first time, I didn't realize what a stressful experience it was going to be. With that in mind, I want to be upfront with you: Your labor and delivery experience will be intense. But don't let that scare you. There are different kinds of stress.

Perhaps a better word for describing the kind of stress you are probably hoping to encounter is the word *eustress*. This word is formed by the addition of the Greek prefix *–eu*, meaning "well" or "good," to the word *stress*. Literally speaking, this changes the word to mean "good stress." The reason I like this word is because we can use it to describe the power that God's goodness can have on your stress.

The important part here is that it is not your job to provide the right attitude to the stress of being in labor in order to make it a positive experience for yourself. You don't have to provide the "good." All you have to do is look for God. Choose to look for His goodness, and He will transform your stressful experience into the good kind.

• **Can you think of another time in your life that should have been stressful, but was transformed into a positive experience because you trusted in God? (Ask God to remind you of a time if you're having difficulty.)**

"The Lord is my rock, my fortress and my deliverer; my God is my rock, in whom I take refuge..." Psalm 18:2

One mistake many women make during labor is depending too heavily on the strength of those around them to get them through. Instead of placing their faith in the true Source of strength, they want to be able to lean on their coach completely. While your husband is going to give you his very best while you are in labor, it is important that you keep your expectations of him in check. He is your coach, not your Savior. Your husband is there to support you, but God is the One who will get you through.

One way to ensure that you will be watching for God during labor is to have scripture prepared to bring with you when you go to the hospital. In the midst of everything going on as your body prepares to give birth to your child, there is something amazing about being in the Word that will help to keep you grounded. Remember, it's not your "inner peace" you need to seek. Ever. It's the Source of peace you need to find.

• Sometime between now and your due date, fill out the section at the back of the book entitled, "Scriptures to Use During Labor." Be sure to bring this book with you when you go into labor.

"Be kind and compassionate to one another, forgiving each other, just as in Christ God forgave you." Ephesians 4:32

After your baby is born and you recount your birth story, it will also be important that you make a point of forgiving each other for any of the tension or disappointments you may have endured together along the way.

• Ask God to help you to forgive each other for any difficulties you may face during labor. Ask God to bring you into parenthood together as a united couple.

• After your baby is born, fill out the worksheet at the end of the book entitled, "Making Your Birth Story a God Story," to help you record God's activity on the day of your child's birth. Then, place the worksheet in your child's baby book.

• **Homework: Pray the following prayer each day.**

"Dear Lord, thank You for providing Your goodness in my childbirth experience. Please help me to perceive Your presence and feel Your peace during my labor experience. In Jesus' name, amen."

WEEK 4

(For Us)

SHARING YOUR BIRTH STORY

"Be wise in the way you act toward outsiders; make the most of every opportunity. Let your conversation always be full of grace, seasoned with salt, so that you may know how to answer everyone." Colossians 4:5-6

I'll never forget the first Christian friend I made in the time following my son's birth. If you can recall, I was being drawn back into a relationship with Christ at that time, and this gal was "on fire for the Lord" in a way I had never seen before. Telling of her life, she would often give replays of conversations she had with God. In these conversations, she would assert that He would tell her various things. She was so matter-of-fact about it: "I said, '_____,' and then God told me, '_____.'"

One day, I finally asked her about it. I couldn't take it anymore. "What do you mean, God said, '_____'? You're telling me you converse with God in an audible way?" I'm pretty sure I didn't actually believe her. But she had my attention.

On the one hand, I thought maybe she was a little crazy. That's just the honest truth. But in all fairness, except for the 'talking to God' thing, she seemed pretty normal. I wondered if maybe she just wanted everyone to see her as "spiritual." Or…maybe she really did talk to God. Maybe she really could hear Him. This option would always linger just a little longer as I pondered her unique ways. I couldn't help but wonder what that would be like. If that last option were true, I rather wished I could experience it, too.

As I think about this young lady, whose life eventually moved her along out of mine, I wonder what my faith journey would have looked like if she had not been there to impact me the way she did. It was brave of her to speak so frankly about her relationship with God around someone who obviously didn't see things the way she did.

When I really think about it, I understand that her words were actually my first experience of 'hearing' God's voice. He spoke to me through her, revealing the kind of relationship He hoped to have with me. He awakened my desire to know Him better. And while I can't audibly hear Him with my ears, my heart has learned the 'sound' of His voice. It was because of that friend that I learned how to really listen.

• **How willing are you to share your faith with others?**

I don't know about you, but sometimes the idea of sharing my faith makes me a little uncomfortable. My story is personal. My story is messy. It runs the risk of having "T.M.I." stamped all over it if I don't share it right. Austin has lovingly offered me some clever advice about the matter. "Let your craziness out a little bit at a time," he'll joke, "that way you won't scare people away." And he's right: While my full testimony of God's deliverance in my life is a powerful one, it's not always the right time to tell it all. Perhaps you can relate.

• **Ask God to give you wisdom and discernment for knowing the right times, places, and words for sharing your faith.**

The beautiful thing here is, whatever your story may be, you're about to have a new one. Once your child is born—however it occurs, and whatever your experience is like—you will have a new story to tell. You will also have a job to do.

"And call upon me in the day of trouble; I will deliver you, and you will honor me." Psalm 50:15

And you will honor me.

Last week, we covered the topic of calling on God during labor. We talked about His R.S.V.P. and the fact that He *will* show up. We covered how, during the birth of your child, you will need to be seeking God's presence whole-heartedly. And then, once your baby is born and God has delivered you from your difficulty and tension into a time of pure joy, then what will you do?

• **Think back on some of the birth stories other people have told you. Did they include God in their story, or was their story about their own ability?**

"Not to us, Lord, not to us but to your name be the glory, because of your love and faithfulness." Psalm 115:1

I once heard a good-hearted Christian woman sum up her birth story with an anecdote of how someone eventually said to her, "You are one powerful woman." And she left it at that. Now, I have no doubt that this woman loves the Lord and tries to seek Him in all her endeavors. And, I'm sure her childbirth experience gave her a whole new respect for what her body was created to do. But when it came to the retelling of her birth story, it seemed to me that she missed the mark. While childbirth is hard work and we women obviously play a *gigantic* role in it, the truth is that without God, none of us would even be here. God is the One who is powerful.

I can't really fault her for telling it like that. Lord knows I'm the same way. (And so are you.) Try as we may to convince ourselves that our hearts are pure toward God, it simply is not true. That's why Jesus came: to save us from our prideful selves.

Each time you tell your story, you will need to choose who will get the glory. Will it be you, or God? Perhaps you are familiar with that law of physics where matter can't be created or destroyed (not by man, anyway) but can only change from one form to another. God's glory is like that. We can't create it. We can't destroy it. But we can *steal* it. And I bet the enemy just loves it when we do.

• **Ask God to make His presence in your birth story undeniable to you, so that you may retell your story accurately and give Him glory each time.**

Where would I be today if my first Christian friend had chosen not to share about her personal experience with God? May you have the boldness to be as matter-of-fact about your experience as my friend was with hers. May your childbirth experience, whatever it ends up looking like, point others directly to the One who got you through it.

The only thing I would like to add here, though it might at first seem contradictory to my plea for you to include God in your story, is that if you forget or even purposely refrain from allowing God to be a character in your birth story, God will love you no less. Remember always, *God's love for you is never based on your performance.* I don't know about you, but when I let that sink in, it makes me want to include Him in my life even more. May it be so for you, too.

• **Ask God to use your child's birth story to reach others.**

• **Homework: Pray the following prayer together this week.**

"Lord, even though our baby hasn't been born yet, we know that You deserve credit for the amazing work You have done and will do in our lives. Please help us to let go of the desire to steal Your glory. Let our story be one that impacts others for Your kingdom. In Jesus' name, amen."

WEEK 4

(For Him)

WHATEVER IS NOBLE

What do I tell new dads? Keep an eye on your wife. Not only does the baby depend on her for everything at first, but she has to give up everything else in order to do it. –Austin

I'll never forget the time Austin came home from work to find me in the rocking chair, holding our screaming baby, and bawling my eyes out.

It was about 6 weeks after our son was born. The meals from friends had run out, the supportive visits from family were over. I was on my own during the day while Austin was at work. But I was on my own at night, too, because I didn't see any point in waking him up so that I could nurse the baby. I really wanted to have it all together. But the truth was I had never been a mom before. I learned as the weeks wore on that it was a lot harder than I expected. I'll never forget the look on Austin's face when he saw me that day. It was one of shocked concern.

Now, don't get me wrong. All the fun stuff was in there, too. We loved having a son. I couldn't believe how quickly Austin became an amazing dad. He was willing to help whenever I asked, and loved playing with his little boy. If the baby's crying ever kept him up at night, he never complained about it. He invited me and the baby to come visit him at work any time. He was as loving and supportive as any husband could possibly be.

The disconnect for us was that he didn't realize motherhood was hard for me. Up until that day when he witnessed my breaking point, he thought I loved every minute. And I did, sort of. But I was also exhausted. As a woman who *really* needs her beauty sleep, the long nights were really taking a toll on me. Everything seemed so much *harder*, mostly because I was sleep-deprived. I kept having this recurring dream that my hands were cuffed in front of me while I was trying to do mundane tasks. For me, that's exactly what it felt like to have a baby in the house. I was dying for Austin to come home from work and say, "Give me the baby. Go take a shower, and go to bed."

• **In what ways are you planning to show support to your wife once your baby is born?**

"But the wisdom that comes from heaven is first of all pure; then peace-loving, considerate, submissive, full of mercy and good fruit, impartial and sincere. Peacemakers who sow in peace reap a harvest of righteousness." James 3:17

When it comes to figuring out what your wife wants, you've probably already learned that if you have to ask, then you're too late. There was a show I watched growing up where the wife said to her baffled husband, "If you don't know what I want, then I'm certainly not going to tell you." Guys, I'm sorry we do that. I truly am. It makes our lives just as hard as it makes yours.

Truth be told, I don't think we always know what we want. Mostly, we just want you to surprise us. We want you to see a need or desire that we haven't even realized yet, and fulfill it. If my husband had said, "What do you need from me right now?" on the day he caught me bawling in the rocking chair, I'm pretty sure my answer would have been a sniffling, "I just don't know!" It wasn't until we were discussing a second child that I was able to make sense of what I had been feeling with the first one.

• How do you usually respond when you don't know what your wife wants from you?

What I can remind you of is that while you aren't likely to ever gain the ability to read your wife's mind, you do have access to pure Wisdom. When you ask God what your wife needs, He will share His wisdom with you. Approach Him with a desire to serve your wife, and see how He blesses you. Remember, you are not alone as the leader of your household. You can trust God to tell you what to do.

• **Ask for God's pure wisdom to help you see your wife's needs once the baby is born. Ask Him to help make this difficult time easier for both of you.**

"Be completely humble and gentle; be patient, bearing with one another in love." Ephesians 4:2

As you move through the postpartum period with your wife, remember that what she needs most is time. As the months go by, you will find that you fall into a new state of normalcy, and the postpartum period will drift into the past as one big blur. As you wait out the difficult postpartum period, you can use the **TIME** acronym to help you remember how else you can help your wife:

TIME

T̲alk. If your wife isn't used to being at home during the day, she may just need you to interact with her as an adult when you come home. She may also need a chance to vent some negative feelings in order for them to go away. Allow her to talk, without judging her or trying to "fix" anything.

I̲ndependence. Like my recurring dream, your wife's hands might feel "bound". Offer her some time to go somewhere with both her hands free. This could be anything from taking a shower or a nap to going shopping without the baby. (This means you'll be alone with the baby for a while. Don't worry, you will do great.)

M̲entor. As hard as you try to be there for your wife, there may still be times that she just needs to be around other women. Encourage her to spend time with other well-meaning mothers, whom she respects and would be interested in learning from and/or growing with. If she doesn't know of anyone, perhaps she could look into joining a Christian mothers group or even a Bible study at your church.

E̲ncouragement. Tell her what a great mom she is and how happy you are to have a family with her. Remind her that the postpartum period is only a season, and that each day will get a little easier.

"Do nothing out of selfish ambition or vain conceit. Rather, in humility value others above yourselves, not looking to your own interests but each of you to the interests of the others." Philippians 2:3-4

As you seek to support your wife throughout the postpartum period (and the rest of your marriage), you will need to keep an eye on yourself, too. Having a new baby isn't just an adjustment period for new moms. After all, most dads in America aren't lucky enough to receive paternity leave. Running on less sleep, you will still be expected to remain competent at work and keep food on the table for as long as your wife stays home. Then, when you come home, you will be expected to help with the baby. That's a tall order. I remember Austin was tired. (He wanted me to tell you that, too.)

During those weeks of "survival" with our second child, we finally found our solution. After work, remembering that this phase of our lives would not last forever, Austin offered to hang out with the baby on the couch—soothing, bouncing, playing, singing, whatever the baby needed—while he watched T.V. and I went up to bed for a few hours. Then he'd wake me at the decided-upon time for the next feeding. I would feed the baby, and we'd all head to bed after that. If the baby fussed or needed me during the night, I felt rested and capable of caring for her. (It's amazing how deeply one can rest in just a few short hours when they are sleep-deprived and they know their baby is in good hands.) Plus, with Austin's offer to help me in that way, I felt so *supported*—which really helped strengthen our relationship, too.

It wasn't always fun to take the baby after a long day at work. But it was what we needed in order to get us through that period.

—Austin

• Ask God to bless your marriage with healthy compromises during the postpartum period. Ask Him to inspire a sense of teamwork between you and your wife.

"Finally, brothers and sisters, whatever is true, whatever is noble, whatever is right, whatever is pure, whatever is lovely, whatever is admirable—if anything is excellent or praiseworthy—think about such things." Philippians 4:8

The last topic we will cover is how to help your wife to be aware of her thoughts. I have spent a lot of time working with the women on this topic, and we've covered in great detail how the setup of your household, her relationship with you, her desired childbirth experience, and even her postpartum period, will all be greatly affected by the thoughts she allows herself to think.

This week, your wife is learning about a phenomenon called *Postpartum Oppression*. To be concise, Postpartum Oppression has to do with the way that new moms try to outdo each other in just about every way. They'll take mental notes all throughout their conversations with each other, discreetly competing for the title of "better mom." These secret battles, complete with judgment of themselves and others, are rampant right now. I had to explain it very clearly to the women, because we don't even realize we're doing it.

The way I've explained it to the ladies is that when it comes to these kinds of conversations, everybody loses. Women who walk away feeling like the better mother, end up tangled up in their own pride. Women who walk away feeling like a big mess end up tripping over feelings of ineptitude. Either way, both walk away feeling a little bit isolated. Isolation is not what God wants for any of us. Postpartum Oppression is a dangerous game that must be avoided in both thought and deed so that your wife can escape from the negative feelings it can cause. It's hard enough to be a new mother. Feeling isolated and judged will only make it worse.

• Ask God to help you identify when Postpartum Oppression is affecting your wife's sense of self-worth. Ask God to help you redirect her attention to finding her worth in Him.

"For we know that in all things God works for the good of those who love him, who have been called according to his purpose." Romans 8:28

As we bring our devotional to a close, I leave you with the reminder that you are not in this alone. Not only do you and your wife have each other, but you also have full access to the power of God Himself. Through prayer and a sincere desire to be in relationship with Him, all the rest of the concerns we have talked about will work themselves out. Keep seeking God's face, and everything will work out for your good. It's God's promise.

Looking back, I know it was God who brought us through. He was there with us. He'll be there with you, too. -Austin

---

• **Homework: Pray the following prayer by yourself each day this week.**

"Dear Lord, I confess that I struggle with trying to take everything on without You. Thank You for loving me anyway. Please continue Your work on my family's structure and in my relationship with my wife. Please let me see You in our childbirth experience, and please use that experience to touch the lives of others. Once I become a new dad, I just ask that You help me to support my wife and find balance in my own life as well. Please bless my marriage and help it to thrive when the baby is born and always. Thank You for this life you have given me. In Jesus' name, amen."

WEEK 4

(For Her)

POSTPARTUM OPPRESSION

**"Am I now trying to win human approval, or God's approval?"
Galatians 1:10**

I have a bone to pick with us women. There's a problem with the way we communicate with each other. For most of you who don't have children yet, you may not even realize the problem exists. But even if you do have children, chances are you're still not fully aware of this issue. Why? Because we women can be sneaky.

It has to do with the way we angle our conversations, in order to discreetly compete against one another. Perhaps the reason we engage in this subtle (yet fierce) form of competition is to try to gain affirmation that we are doing a good job as mothers. After all, parenting is hard. It's a job where you don't receive concrete feedback about your efforts until many years down the road. The problem is that as mothers, when we seek to gain affirmation by trying to outperform each other, all we are really doing is holding each other down. (And holding someone's face in the mud is no way to climb to the top.) I call this way of interacting between mothers *Postpartum Oppression.*

"The mouth of the righteous is a fountain of life, but the mouth of the wicked conceals violence." Proverbs 10:11

After your child is born, you will probably find that multitudes of other women will be drawn to you and your baby. There will be plenty of older mothers, who will gaze at your baby and reminisce about their own children who are now grown. These precious women mean you no harm. But there will also be plenty of younger mothers who are drawn to you, and to be honest, it's not always out of fondness for you or your adorable baby.

Some women seek to compete with every new mother they meet, while others save it for their closest mother friends. Some are open about feeling competitive toward other moms, and others keep their thoughts to themselves (but think them, nonetheless.) There are all kinds of different subject matter for these competitions, depending on what each mother deems important.

For example, some new mothers only want to compare childbirth experiences. (For most of these women, either the most "natural" or the "shortest" birth usually wins.) For others, it might be the topics of nursing, working, diapering, sleep schedules, weight loss, or even brand of baby strollers. Keep tabs on the conversations you hear between new mothers, and you'll see that it is often a verbal score board where the mothers judge themselves against each other.

• **Ask God to give you an understanding of what Postpartum Oppression is. Ask Him to help you see why engaging in it is unwise.**

"Do not let any unwholesome talk come out of your mouths, but only what is helpful for building others up according to their needs, that it may benefit those who listen." Ephesians 4:29

The tricky part about Postpartum Oppression is that you will do it others, and it will be done to you—unless you are aware of it. If you find yourself measuring your performance against another mother, then you are both a perpetrator and a victim of Postpartum Oppression. This involves your thoughts as much as it involves your actions.

You need to be aware of how you feel upon leaving each conversation with other moms. Ask yourself: 'Do I feel like I'm a better mom than her?' 'Do I feel like she's a better mom than me?' If you find yourself answering 'yes' to either of these questions, it's a red flag that Postpartum Oppression has taken place. When you compare yourself to others, you are setting yourself up for a dangerous game which the enemy can, and will, use against you. You'll either end up tangled up in your own pride, or tripping over feelings of ineptitude. Either way, you lose.

• **Ask God to give you the self-control to neither initiate, nor participate in, Postpartum Oppression.**

"But encourage one another day after day, as long as it is still called 'Today,' so that none of you may be hardened by sin's deceitfulness." Hebrews 3:13

Last summer, I took my children to the zoo. Having finally arrived at a shady place to pull my daughter out of her stroller, I picked her up and held her so we could look at the gorilla exhibit. As we stood there, the most amazing thing happened. The mother gorilla looked up at us through the glass, and in two large, sweeping steps, like a very graceful linebacker carrying a football, she brought her tiny, furry, *humanlike* newborn right up to the glass in front of me. There we stood, she and I, for quite some time. Just two mothers, holding our babies. There was no comparison of how our babies had been born, or which milestones they had reached at certain ages. Instead, we were connected in a mutual awe of motherhood. It was simple and beautiful. As I walked away, I was filled with amazement at God's incredible ability to create life.

That's what it should be like between us women. We should be focusing on what we have in common during this challenging and rewarding period of life. We should be helping each other to laugh, to shake off the seriousness of parenthood so that we can enjoy our children. We should be connecting in friendship, reminding each other that our worth comes from God alone—not from whether or not we choose to allow our children to have pacifiers.

When you become a new mother, the other mothers you interact with should walk away feeling free, relieved of the pressure to outperform you. They should be smiling. They should be wondering, Christian and non-Christian alike, what it must be like to find their worth in God and whether He was part of *their* birth story. They should leave with a sense of wonder and gratitude for the life they are living. This is what God has called us to do.

• **Ask God to fill you with wonder and gratitude after your baby is born.**

"Finally, brothers and sisters, whatever is true, whatever is noble, whatever is right, whatever is pure, whatever is lovely, whatever is admirable—if anything is excellent or praiseworthy—think about such things." Philippians 4:8

Along the same lines as how to treat other mothers once your baby comes, is the question of how to treat your husband. As you encounter the postpartum period (often referred to as the "fourth trimester") it will also be important that you pay particular attention to the way you think about him. The postpartum period can be difficult for women because the baby seems to depend so heavily upon us—especially during those first twelve weeks. Whether our babies are breastfed or bottle-fed, sometimes it can feel like there's little our husbands can do to help us. And after a few weeks without sleep, our thoughts can sometimes run away with us.

When it comes to your husband, he might need direction from you regarding what the baby needs. He might also need you to tell him what *you* need. Now, I know it's not much fun to have to tell someone what you want for your birthday. But this isn't your birthday. This is your marriage, and your husband is on your team. Don't make him play the guessing game.

I have provided your husband with what I hope will be enough ammunition to at least help him communicate his desire to help you. But the rest is up to you. Ask for his help, and then accept it. His parenting might not look just like yours, but that's ok. Your baby will thrive on the extra stimulation. Most importantly, if you start to feel like you're the one doing all the work, and you start to feel resentful, you'll need to keep yourself in check. Remember that both of you are new to parenthood. Sometimes, it helps to remind yourself that you don't always know what you're doing, either.

• Ask God to protect your state of mind, and your marriage, during the postpartum period. Ask Him to help you extend grace to each other as you work toward finding your "new normal."

"How good and pleasant it is when God's people dwell together in unity!" Psalm 133:1

Lastly, remember that your husband will also have a lot to handle when the baby comes. Although his hands might not be full with your little bundle of joy all of the time, he will probably be returning to work long before you do. That means he'll be burning the candle at both ends, with high expectations of him wherever he turns. Remember to ask him how he's doing, too. Remember to ask him what he needs. Remember that someday, when your darling child is grown and gone, you plan to still be married to him. That means you'll need to look out for him, too.

• Ask God to help you remember how important your husband is to you, especially after the baby is born. Ask Him to help your relationship to thrive.

"But seek first his kingdom and his righteousness, and all these things will be given to you as well." Matthew 6:33

It's time for you to go forth and become a Mom. As you do, my greatest desire is for you to always remember that nothing you do, say, think, or feel will determine your worth as a woman, mother, or person. Your worth comes from God alone. He loves you and accepts you always. Through prayer and a sincere desire to be in relationship with Him, all the rest of the concerns we have talked about will work themselves out. Keep watch over your motives, allowing nothing to replace God as the source of your worth. Seek God's voice, and rest assured that you are going to be just fine. Congratulations on becoming a mother!

• **Homework: Pray the following prayer by yourself each day this week.**

"Dear Lord, I confess that I try to gain worth from numerous things besides You. Thank you for loving me anyway. Once I become a new mother, please soften my heart toward other mothers. Eliminate in me the need to compete. Please use me as a vessel to show Your love, encouraging those in need, showing my vulnerabilities, and never making other women feel worse about themselves. Please bless my marriage and help it to thrive when the baby is born and always. Thank You for this life You have given me. In Jesus' name, amen."

SCRIPTURES TO USE DURING LABOR

Look up each of the following verses and record them here. Be sure to bring these verses with you to the hospital so you can reflect on them during labor.

2 Chronicles 15:7

Psalms 28:7

Psalms 37:4

Psalms 46:12

Psalms 86:6-7

Psalms 139:14

1 John 5:14-15

Hebrews 4:16

John 14:13

John 16:21

Isaiah 26:3-4

Isaiah 40:30

Isaiah 41:10

Isaiah 43:2

Isaiah 43:13

Romans 5:3-5

Ephesians 3:20

Philippians 3:13-14

Deuteronomy 31:6

James 1:22

2 Peter 3:9

1 John 4:18

Joshua 1:9

Additional verses for postpartum and beyond:

Psalms 37:4

Isaiah 30:21

Ephesians 3:20-21

RECORDING YOUR CHILD'S BIRTH STORY

The Birth Story of:

Date and Time of Birth:

Who was present:

What we were doing when labor started:

How it progressed:

What Mom remembers most:

What Dad remembers most:

When we prayed, and what for:

What scriptures we used:

How God answered our prayers:

Other measures we used for comfort:

Anything else we want to be sure to remember:

Thank God for His presence during your child's birth. Acknowledge the ways He answered your prayers.

EXPECTANT PARENTS WORKSHOP

ABOUT JENNIFER DEBRITO, CCLD, CCBE

Jennifer DeBrito, CCLD, CCBE is a Colorado Native and has lived in Colorado Springs since 1998. She holds a Bachelor of Science degree in Natural Health, and is also certified as a Christian Labor Doula and Christian Birth Educator. She is the proud owner of Eden's Promise, LLC, and a volunteer educator at the Colorado Springs Pregnancy Center. She is married with two children (and two birth stories) of her own.

Made in the USA
Monee, IL
11 December 2021